Mysterious Monsters

Searching for UFOs

Jennifer Rivkin

PowerKiDS
press
New York

Published in 2015 by The Rosen Publishing Group, Inc.
29 East 21st Street, New York, NY 10010

Produced for Rosen by BlueApple*Works* Inc.
Art Director: Tibor Choleva
Designer: Joshua Avramson
Photo Research: Jane Reid
Editor for BlueApple*Works*: Melissa McClellan
US Editor: Joshua Shadowens

Illustrations: Cover J. Avramson; p. 1 background Triff/Shutterstock; p. 1 welcomia/Shutterstock; p. 4, 20 top Chromatika Multimedia snc/Shutterstock; p. 4 background Vadim Sadovski/Shutterstock; p. 6 background orin/Shutterstock; p. 7 background orin/Shutterstock; p. 7 right ArchieMkDesign/Shutterstock; p. 8 top Fotokostic/Shutterstock; p. 8-9 background red-feniks/Shutterstock; p. 10 background J. Avramson; p. 15 right Photobank gallery/Shutterstock; p. 16 top right Alex Mit/Shutterstock; p. 22-23 background diversepixel/Shutterstock; p. 22 top M. Cornelius/Shutterstock; p. 23 right Linda Bucklin/Shutterstock; p. 24-25 background njaj/Shutterstock; p. 24 top solarseven/Shutterstock; p. 26 top Angela Harburn/Shutterstock; p. 28-29 background M. Cornelius/shutterstock; p. 28 top Vadim Sadovski/Shutterstock

Photo Credits: Back Cover njaj/Shutterstock; p. 6, 13, 24 NASA; p. 8 right ESA; p. 9, 10 top, 10, 19, 22, 25 Fortean Picture Library; p. 11 left Valentin Armianu/Dreamstime; p. 11 right Zrfphoto/Dreamstime; p. 12-13 background schmaelterphoto/Shutterstock; p. 12 top bikeriderlondon/Shutterstock; p. 12 left Marius Sipa/Dreamstime; p. 12 right Alexey Stiop/Dreamstime; p. 14 top Fer Gregory/Shutterstock; p. 14 Jabberocky/Public Domain; p. 15 Deveomedia; p. 16-17 background Berti123/Shutterstock; p. 16 top OSalenko/Shutterstock; p. 16 public domain; p. 17 left Blagov58/Dreamstime; p. 17 right Larry Gevert/Dreamstime; p. 18-19 background Samuel Borges Photography/Shutterstock; p. 18 top Dejan Stanisavljevic/Shutterstock; p. 19 right Chris Curtis/Shutterstock; p. 20 Kathy Burns-millyard/Dreamstime; p. 21 Phil Mcdonald/Dreamstime; p. 26 Featureflash/Shutterstock; p. 27 Andrey Bayda/Shutterstock; paper background Fedorov Oleksiy/Shutterstock; p. 28 bottom left to right, Edyta Pawlowska/Shutterstock, Helder Almeida/Shutterstock, Pete Pahham/Shutterstock

Library of Congress Cataloging-in-Publication-Data

Rivkin, Jennifer, author.
 Searching for UFOs / by Jennifer Rivkin.
    pages cm. — (Mysterious monsters)
Includes index.
ISBN 978-1-4777-7109-9 (library binding) — ISBN 978-1-4777-7110-5 (pbk.) —
ISBN 978-1-4777-7111-2 (6-pack)
1. Unidentified flying objects—Juvenile literature. 2. Unidentified flying objects—Sightings and encounters—Juvenile literature. I. Title. II. Title: Searching for unidentified flying objects.
TL789.2.R58 2015
001.942—dc23
                              2014003104

Manufactured in the United States of America

CPSIA Compliance Information: Batch #WS14PK8 For Further Information contact: Rosen Publishing, New York, New York at 1-800-237-9932

TABLE OF CONTENTS

WHAT IS A UFO?

From the beginning of recorded history—and maybe even longer—people have reported seeing unexplainable objects in the sky. They have seen bright lights, colorful egg-shaped objects, or metallic looking discs hurtling through the clouds. In the 1940s, enough people saw the disc-like objects that they became widely known as flying saucers.

Unidentified Flying Objects

The US Air Force **coined** the term Unidentified Flying Objects (UFOs) in 1953 to include **airborne** objects of any shape. The air force was interested in UFOs for national security reasons. They wanted to know if the objects posed any danger to US citizens. Were they enemy aircraft? **Stellar** objects? Visitors from another planet? The military defined UFOs as "any airborne object, which does not conform to any presently known aircraft or missile type, or which cannot be positively identified as a familiar object."

IS THERE LIFE OUT THERE?

The observable universe is billions of **light-years** wide. Some scientists think that it could be even larger, maybe infinite. The planets in our solar system are just a tiny fraction of what is out there. Using powerful telescopes, scientists from The National Aeronautics and Space Administration **(NASA)** have recently discovered thousands of planets outside of our solar system that **orbit** distant stars, like Earth orbits the Sun.

▲ This is a scale model of the Kepler spacecraft. Using this spacecraft scientists have discovered six Earth-like planets orbiting a Sun-like star, called Kepler-11. These planets are about 2,000 light-years from Earth.

GOLDILOCKS PLANETS

In 2009, researchers at NASA launched the *Kepler* spacecraft to search for Earth-sized planets around other stars. Over 100 of the planets that they have found are about the same distance away from their stars as Earth is from the Sun. Scientists refer to these as Goldilocks Planets— not too hot, not too cold, just right for life as we know it. These discoveries are bringing scientists another step closer to determining if there could be other life in the universe.

▶ *Do you think that Earth is the only place in the universe with intelligent life? Or, is it more likely that someone—or something—else is out there? Perhaps other forms of intelligent life have been searching for us, the same way that we have been to searching for them. Maybe they have already found us!*

DID YOU KNOW?

The Hubble Space Telescope, which orbits Earth and beams images back, was launched in 1990. It takes 97 minutes for Hubble to orbit the globe. The telescope circles at 353 miles (568 km) above Earth's surface so that its pictures are not affected by Earth's atmosphere. The information from Hubble is important for scientists. Hubble has helped scientists understand how galaxies form and how planets are born.

FIRST SIGHTINGS

Some researchers say that ancient Egyptian hieroglyphs show evidence of UFOs. In 329 BC, it is said that Alexander the Great (a Greek king) saw two large silver shields with fire around the rims, diving at his army from the sky. In 1897, thousands of people across the US claimed to have seen UFOs in the sky. In 1909, a number of sightings took place in Australia and New Zealand. There have been eyewitness accounts on all continents.

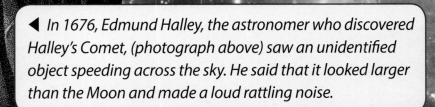

◄ In 1676, Edmund Halley, the astronomer who discovered Halley's Comet, (photograph above) saw an unidentified object speeding across the sky. He said that it looked larger than the Moon and made a loud rattling noise.

A Newsworthy Sighting

One of the most famous UFO sightings occurred in 1947. Pilot Kenneth Arnold reported that he saw nine shiny unidentified objects flying in a diagonal pattern near Mount Rainer, Washington. Arnold estimated that the objects, which were shaped like discs, were flying over 1,200 mph (1,930 km/h). This was three times faster than any manned plane that was available at the time. The media got hold of the information, and the story captured the nation's attention.

In 1904, US Navy Lieutenant Frank Schofield of the USS *Supply* in San Francisco claimed to have seen three giant, red, egg-shaped objects flying in formation. Schofield, along with two crew members, said they watched the airborne objects for a full two minutes.

▶ *Arnold shows a drawing of the object he saw. He seemed to be a credible witness. He was a respected businessperson and pilot. Over a dozen other UFO sightings were reported in Washington on the day that Arnold said that he saw the nine objects in the sky.*

Gen. Ramey Empties Roswell Saucer

Lewis Pushes Advantage in New Con...

Sheriff Wilcox Takes Leading Role in Excitement Over Report 'Saucer' Found

Arrest 2,000 In Athens in...

Send First Roswell Wire Photos from Record Office

Ramey Says Excitement Is Not Justified

General Ramey Says Disk Is Weather Balloon

Southern... Only Hold... In New Co...

Roswell UFO Crash

It was a big year for UFOs in 1947. The same year that Arnold reported his sighting, William (Mac) Brazel noticed large areas of **debris** on a ranch where he was working in Roswell, New Mexico. Government officials said that the wreckage was from a weather balloon that hit the ground.

Not everyone is convinced that the government was telling the truth. Some people now believe that what crashed that day in Roswell was actually a UFO occupied by aliens. They think that the military captured the **extraterrestrials** to study them and then covered up the actual events with the weather balloon story.

◀ Military personnel collecting the debris after the Roswell crash.

US Military Balloon, Not Aliens

In 1947, military personnel showed off a weather balloon crash to reporters (foil, rubber, and wood), and no one questioned it. Then, in 1978, scientist, Stanton T. Friedman interviewed Major Jesse Marcel who had been involved in the debris recovery after the crash. He made the claim of a cover up. Researchers have put together hundreds of government documents about the case. After the alien reports, the government investigated. Officials then said that a US Air Force surveillance balloon, which had been a top-secret experiment at the time, was the object that crashed. They say that anyone who says that the crash involved aliens is either carrying out a **hoax** or has confused memories.

▶ Whether or not the alien cover up theory is true, Roswell hasn't been the same since the crash. The town even has a UFO museum. Exhibits include information on the incident, UFO sightings, and alien abductions. If you visit in early July, you'll be there for the town's annual Roswell UFO Festival.

AREA 51

Roswell is not the only location that is **shrouded** in UFO-related mystery. Area 51 in the Nevada desert shares a similar reputation. Area 51 is a restricted US Air Force military base. It is not on public maps. If you did happen to come across Area 51 in the desert, you would find it surrounded by motion detectors, fences, and security guards. Some say that experimental weapons and aircraft are developed and tested at the site. The government is extremely secretive about Area 51.

WARNING

Restricted Area

WARNING!
NO TRESPASSING
AUTHORITY N.R.S. 207-200
MAXIMUM PUNISHMENT: $1000 FINE
SIX MONTHS IMPRISONMENT
OR BOTH
STRICTLY ENFORCED

WARNING
MILITARY INSTALLATION

IT IS UNLAWFUL TO ENTER THIS INSTALLATION WITHOUT
THE WRITTEN PERMISSION OF THE INSTALLATION COMMANDER.

INSTALLATION COMMANDER
AUTHORITY: Internal Security Act, 50
U.S.C. 797
PUNISHMENT: Up to one year imprisonment
or $5,000. fine.

PHOTOGRAPHY
OF THIS AREA
IS PROHIBITED

ENTERING AREA 51

◀ *Some people believe that the government is hiding underground experiments taking place at Area 51—studies of UFOs, aliens, and extraterrestrial technology. Could military officials be taking UFOs apart then putting them back together to figure out how they work? This procedure is called reverse engineering.*

Human Made UFOs at Area 51

No one can be sure that anything extraterrestrial has gone on at the base, but man-made "UFOs" have definitely been there. In 2013, the government made previously secret documents available to the public. These declassified papers showed that both the U-2 spy plane and OXCART surveillance aircraft were tested at Area 51 in the 1950s and 60s. This may have been one of the reasons for so many UFO sightings at the time.

▲ *Many planes tested at Area 51 are new and innovative. People seeing them flying by for the first time might believe they came from outer space. It is probably not a coincidence that a lot of UFO sightings come from places with airbases nearby.*

CLOSE ENCOUNTERS

Thousands of UFO sightings were reported during the 1950s and 1960s. **UFOlogists** had no way to analyze or sort them until Dr. Allen Hynek developed a method in 1972. Dr. Hynek became the first UFOlogist to categorize UFO events and divide them into different types of close encounters. UFOlogists now classify all UFO events according to his categories, from close encounters of the first kind to close encounters of the sixth kind.

▼ *In the 1980s, crop circles began to appear all over the world, especially in Great Britain and Japan. UFOlogists suggested they were made by landing spacecraft.*

Close Encounter (CE) Categories

CE 1: Sighting a UFO only

CE 2: Finding some physical evidence left by a UFO or alien

CE 3: Sighting alien(s)

CE 4: Being abducted by aliens

CE 5: Humans and aliens meet and interact

CE 6: An animal or human dies during a meeting with aliens

ALIEN ABDUCTIONS

A recent US survey suggests that many people believe they have been abducted by aliens. Some victims reportedly only realize they have been abducted after their memories are drawn out through regression therapy. In this type of therapy, a therapist hypnotizes a person to help him or her relive past events. One UFOlogist claims we all may have been abducted at one time or another—we just may not remember it!

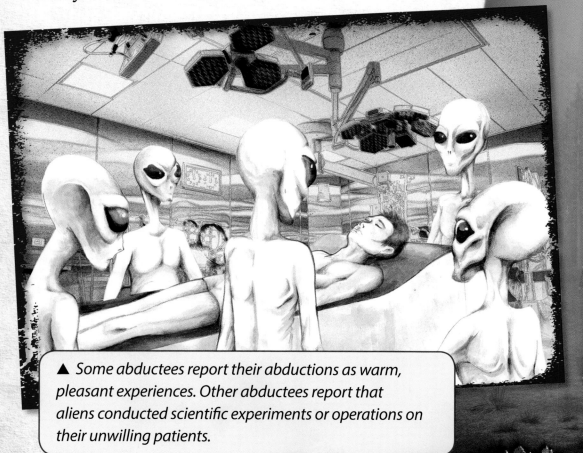

▲ Some abductees report their abductions as warm, pleasant experiences. Other abductees report that aliens conducted scientific experiments or operations on their unwilling patients.

STRANGE LIGHTS

In 1561, citizens of Nuremberg, Germany, awoke to a frightening (or awesome) sight in the sky. According to reports, many people watched as two red crescents appeared in the middle of the Sun. Then they saw bright spheres, cylinders, and other shapes that seemed to "battle" in the sky above them for over an hour. Some UFO buffs call this the "UFO Battle over Nuremberg." A woodcut artwork from Hans Glaser illustrated the events. Those who believe in ancient UFOs consider this a piece of evidence.

◄ Glaser's woodcut shows the events that occurred in Nuremberg in 1561. Was it really a fight between alien spacecraft? Perhaps the woodcut is more a religious interpretation (there were crosses in the picture) and not an exact image of what people saw that day. On the other hand some researches say that the crosses might represent the shape of the airplane-like flying objects.

Natural Phenomenon

If there were lights in the sky that day, there are other explanations from Mother Nature. One idea is that the lights could have been ball lightning, which occurs during thunderstorms, usually after a lightning strike. These floating fireballs can be different colors (white, yellow, orange, red, or blue). The strange balls of light could also have been sun dogs, an atmospheric event that creates rings or bright spots beside the Sun. Comets or meteors are another explanation.

▶ Studies show that most UFO sightings are misidentified natural phenomena or objects like aircraft, clouds, comets, or meteors. For example, lenticular clouds are shaped like a UFO. They form in the troposphere, the part of the atmosphere closest to Earth. Scientists believe these clouds explain some UFO sightings.

GOVERNMENT STUDIES

The government is interested in UFOs for many reasons, but mostly for national security. They want to know if the flying objects pose a threat to their citizens. Government researchers need to determine whether the objects are natural phenomena or whether they are military aircraft from other nations—or from other parts of the universe.

One of the first studies of UFOs that the government shared with the public took place after the Kenneth Arnold sighting in 1947. The US Air Force's Project Sign lasted a year. Officially, the project did not find evidence of extraterrestrial UFOs.

Did You Know?

In 2011, many US citizens signed a petition requesting the government to formally acknowledge an extraterrestrial presence on Earth. In response to the petition, the White House put out the following press release: "Thank you for signing the petition asking the Obama Administration to acknowledge an extraterrestrial presence here on Earth. The US government has no evidence that any life exists outside our planet, or that an extraterrestrial presence has contacted or engaged any member of the human race. In addition, there is no credible information to suggest that any evidence is being hidden from the public's eye."

Is the Government Hiding Something?

In 1951, Edward Ruppelt led the air force study called Project Blue Book for a short time. He was said to be more open-minded about the possibility of extraterrestrials. Project Blue Book found that 69 percent of sightings were misidentifications, 22 percent were unknown (UFOs), and the researchers were unable to make a determination about the rest. In 1970, Project Blue Book was shut down and its files were made available to the public. But more recent documents related to UFOs are still classified. What secrets could they hold?

▲ Lieutenant Colonel Hector Quintanilla Jr. (middle) led the Project Blue Book investigation team from 1963–1970. The team collected, analyzed, and filed thousands of UFO reports. In 1968, the Condon Report said the government should not keep studying UFOs. Project Blue Book was shut down in 1970. Still, according to a recent survey by National Geographic, 79 percent of people think that the government has kept information about UFOs a secret from the public. What do you think?

UFO Organizations

Some people are not happy to just sit back and wait for the government to provide information on UFOs. Dozens of organizations are trying to discover the truth for themselves.

One of the scientists who worked on Project Blue Book formed his own agency. Dr. Allen Hynek created the Center for UFO Studies (CUFOS) because he believed that some of the sightings that he studied while working on Blue Book were unexplainable.

The Center for the Search for ExtraTerrestrial Intelligence (SETI) searches for evidence of intelligent life in the universe by looking for signs of otherworldly technology. They are looking for signals from advanced technological civilizations in our galaxy.

UFO Festivals

If you are interested in UFOs, you are not alone. Every year, thousands of UFO enthusiasts across the US get together to share information and have fun at festivals. Roswell holds a three-day event that has guest speakers, authors, live entertainment, a costume contest, a pet costume contest, and a parade.

The McMenamins UFO Festival in Oregon has guest speakers as well as live music. The Bridgefest UFO Festival in Bridgeville, California, has a flying saucer contest. Teams throw homemade UFOs over the bridge and get points for distance, accuracy, style, and looks.

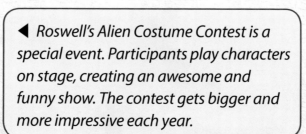

◀ *Roswell's Alien Costume Contest is a special event. Participants play characters on stage, creating an awesome and funny show. The contest gets bigger and more impressive each year.*

HOAXES & MISUNDERSTANDINGS

The government's Project Blue Book study determined that about eight percent of UFO sightings were hoaxes. To get attention, or just to have fun, some people play pranks to try and get others to believe that they have evidence of UFOs. They often take videos or pictures.

Back when there were no laptops and no iPods, the pranksters making fake UFO videos had to do it the old-fashioned way. Using creativity (and craft glue), they tried anything to get a realistic-looking photo. Some used tinfoil-covered Frisbees thrown in the air. Others used small hot-air balloons or the hubcap from a child's wagon wheel.

◀ *Back then, it was trickier to get a great shot of a fake UFO, and it was easier to spot a fake one. This fake photo was taken after a coat button was thrown in the air.*

ALMOST REAL FAKES

Today, the reverse is true. Faking a photo is much easier and spotting a fraud may be next to impossible. Photo editing programs make it easy to change images. Videos are becoming more common, too.

In the 1990s, British businessman Ray Santilli released videos that he claimed were of alien autopsies taken at Roswell. It was big news at the time since the footage appeared to be real. In 2006, Santilli admitted that the film was a fake.

▶ *The best fake images and films use computer-generated images (CGI), like the ones used in Hollywood films. When you go to a science fiction movie, you know you are going to be seeing something created from the director's imagination.*

THE SCIENTISTS' VIEW

Most scientists are skeptical that eyewitness accounts of UFOs are the result of actual ships from outer space. Sightings can often be explained. A few are hoaxes. Most are likely misidentifications.

In the 1950s and 1960s, many sightings were later explained by the U-2 plane making test flights. The military is secretive about testing, so the public doesn't always know about advances in military or weapons technology.

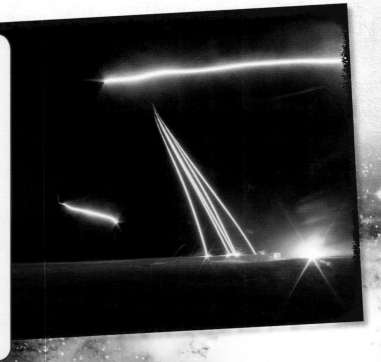

▶ The air force training maneuvers can definitely look like a UFO attack! In 2008, a UFO report was so convincing that it was picked up by the media. In this mass sighting, 40 witnesses in Stephensville, Texas, saw bright soundless lights that moved in strange patterns and were being pursued by military planes. Eventually, the air force explained that they were flying F-16 training maneuvers and dropping flares suspended on parachutes.

On Alien Abductions

What about the tens of thousands of people who claim to have been captured by aliens for medical testing? Scientists believe that most are not mentally ill, nor are they lying. Many people truly believe that they have been abducted by aliens. In fact, one study showed that when they recalled the events, their heart rates rose and they began to sweat, just like people who have been through a traumatic experience. Still, only a small **minority** of scientists think that the "**abductees**" are remembering something that actually happened.

Eyewitness Tale

In 1976, Chuck Foltz, Charles Rack, and Jim and Jack Weiner say they were taken from their canoe as they floated on Eagle Lake in the Allagash Wilderness Waterway. First, they saw a bright orb. Then they were taken aboard an alien spacecraft and used as human test subjects by four-fingered aliens. When they got back to their campsite, they felt that they had been gone for only minutes. The size of the fire let them know that they had been away for two hours. The four men later recalled the events while under **hypnosis**.

▶ Alan Godfrey, an abductee from England, talks about his ordeal. Most scientists find that people who claim to have been abducted do so because they have heard stories of abductions before and either dreamed or fantasized them in a way that seemed real.

UFOs In Popular Culture

The idea of UFOs stimulates people's imaginations. It's exciting to think that there are other intelligent life forms in the universe, and that they may want to make contact with us. It is not surprising that UFOs and aliens have been the main characters in many books, TV shows, and movies.

A quick search of the Internet comes up with thousands of books on UFOs alone. UFOs and aliens are popular on the small screen, too. Fictional programs like *Star Trek* and *Roswell* had people seeing aliens. *The X-Files* TV series, in which FBI agents examine unsolved cases involving **paranormal** occurrences, often featured aliens in the plot.

◀ *Actors David Duchovny and Gillian Anderson star in the movie* The X-Files, *based on their popular TV series. FBI Agent Fox Mulder (Duchovny) believed in aliens and UFOs, while Agent Dana Scully (Anderson) was more skeptical. The TV series and movie were about extraterrestrials and conspiracy theories.*

Movies

In 1977, Stephen Spielberg's *Close Encounters of the Third Kind* renewed interest in UFOs. It also got people thinking about government conspiracies to keep the public in the dark about aliens. In 1982, Spielberg made aliens seem more adorable in *E.T.: The Extra-Terrestrial.*

More recent films have brought back the paranoia. The 1996 film *Independence Day* featured aliens coming to invade and destroy planet Earth.

Men in Black, a 1997 film, hit on the government conspiracy idea. In the popular film, Will Smith and Tommy Lee Jones play government agents who supervise extraterrestrial life forms on Earth. Their job is to keep the aliens' existence a secret from ordinary civilians.

Did You Know?

A film festival celebrating all things UFO takes place in Arizona. Hosted by the International UFO Congress, the festival presents movie awards for categories, such as: Best UFO Documentary, Best Abductee Documentary, and Best UFO Footage within a Documentary.

▲ *Will Smith is one of the stars of the* Men in Black *movie series. The movies follow Agents J and K as they try to protect the world from aliens who are living on Earth and trying to destroy it.*

IS THE TRUTH OUT THERE?

Every day, new UFO sightings are reported. In 2013, a 61-year-old woman from Morgan Hill, California, claimed to have seen three UFOs above the horizon. All three were in a row but had differing brightness. The one in the middle was the most luminous. The woman looked at the objects through binoculars and noticed that there was a red beacon on the top and a dome-like shape underneath. There were yellow-orange lights that looked like "ribs" around the outside.

Many eyewitnesses are regular, trustworthy people. Could they all be wrong? Over a third of Americans don't think so.

▼ *A recent survey by National Geographic found that 36 percent of Americans believe that UFOs are real. Are you one of them?*

THE BOTTOM LINE

Just because most UFO sightings have earthly explanations, that doesn't mean there isn't intelligent life somewhere in the universe. In fact, in 2011, when the government responded to the citizen petition for information if extraterrestrial life exists, they acknowledged that no one yet knows for sure. Many scientists and mathematicians have looked at the question of whether life likely exists beyond Earth. They have come to the conclusion that the odds are pretty high that somewhere among the trillions of stars in the universe there is a planet other than ours that is home to life.

GLOSSARY

abductees (ab-duck-TEEZ) People taken away from a place by force.

airborne (EHR-born) Being in the air.

coined (KOIND) To create a new word or phrase that other people begin to use.

debris (duh-BREE) The pieces that are left after something has been destroyed.

extraterrestrials (ek-struh-teh-RES-tree-ulz) Originating, existing, or occurring outside the earth or its atmosphere.

hoax (HOHKS) To trick into believing or accepting as genuine something false and often preposterous.

hypnosis (hip-NOH-sus) A trancelike state that resembles sleep but is induced by a person whose suggestions are readily accepted by the subject.

light-years (LYT-yeerz) A unit of length in astronomy equal to the distance that light travels in one year in a vacuum or about 5.88 trillion miles (9.46 trillion kilometers).

minority (my-NOR-ih-tee) A number or amount that is less than half of a total.

NASA (NAH-suh) The National Aeronautics and Space Administration (the agency of the United States government that is responsible for the civilian space program and for aeronautics and aerospace research).

orbs (ORBZ) Something (such as a planet, the Sun, or the Moon) that is shaped like a ball.

paranormal (pa-ruh-NOR-mul) Not scientifically explainable.

stellar (STEH-lur) Of or relating to the stars.

UFOlogists (yoo-ef-AH-luh-jistz) People who study unidentified flying objects.

FOR MORE INFORMATION

FURTHER READING

Cheatham, Mark. *Aliens!* Jr. Graphic Monster Stories. New York: PowerKids Press, 2012.

Pipe, Jim. *Aliens.* The Twilight Realm. New York: Gareth Stevens, 2013.

Webb, Stuart. *Alien Encounters.* Paranormal Files. New York: Rosen Publishing Group, 2012.

WEBSITES

Due to the changing nature of Internet links, PowerKids Press has developed an online list of websites related to the subject of this book. This site is updated regularly. Please use this link to access the list:

www.powerkidslinks.com/mymo/ufo/

INDEX